Bryce Canyon
National Park

impressions

photography by James Randklev
foreword by Greer K. Chesher

FARCOUNTRY
PRESS

RIGHT: Known as the Silent City, Bryce Amphitheater is awe-inspiring.

TITLE PAGE: Bryce Canyon National Park follows the edge of the Paunsaugunt Plateau. On the west are forested tablelands.

FRONT COVER: Morning light sets Agua Canyon aglow.

BACK COVER: Thor's Hammer is one of Bryce Canyon's most popular hoodoos. It is named for the Norse god of thunder.

ISBN 10: 1-56037-251-6
ISBN 13: 978-1-56037-251-6

© 2003 by Farcountry Press
Photography © 2003 by James Randklev

For more information about our books, write Farcountry Press, P.O. Box 5630, Helena, MT 59604; call (800) 821-3874; or visit www.farcountrypress.com.

Created, produced, and designed in the United States.
Printed in China.

5   14   13   12   11   2   3   4   5   6   7

ABOVE: A young ponderosa pine is dwarfed below giant hoodoos in Queen's Garden.

FACING PAGE: Early morning light warms the eroded cliffs at Rainbow Point.

Foreword

by Greer K. Chesher

A breeze almost imperceptibly blows along the rim of Bryce Canyon. Below, in the drowsy slumber of a late summer afternoon, row upon row of hoodoos stand like terracotta warriors in a Chinese emperor's tomb. Not a sound breaks the silence; ravens wheel overhead, a yellow-bellied marmot peeks from a cliff-edge perch while the sun pours down on the last living branch of a 1,600-year-old bristlecone pine, the essence of minimalism.

Although it may not look it, Bryce Canyon is a world in motion. Daily, from seemingly immutable cliffs rocks tumble, ancient and immovable hoodoos shed skin, and high-angled slopes elbow downhill. Underfoot, the very soil ripples as unseen microorganisms tunnel gossamer fingers. The silent forest bustles as mule deer, prairie dog, coyote, hawk, and snake partner in life's dynamic and complex dance. Bryce began, lives, and will fade away in motion.

Sixty million years ago, the land that would become Bryce embraced a large inland lake near sea level much like today's Lake Michigan. Over the next 10 million years the lake imbibed what vibrant rivers offered: silt, clay, and mud. During droughts, howling deserts blew across the lake's dry bed. Sediments stacked and hardened into alternating limestones, mudstones, and sandstones now known as the Claron Formation.

Fifteen million years ago deep geologic forces heaved the Colorado Plateau, an area roughly the

size of Utah but centered on the Four Corners, more than two miles (three kilometers) above sea level. The massive plateau cracked and splintered, leaving smaller plateaus jumbled at differing elevations. The elegant Claron capped three of these plateaus: the Markagunt where Cedar Breaks National Monument's pottery spires radiate evening sun; the Aquarius from which Powell Point, seen opposite Bryce, erodes; and the Paunsaugunt where the delicate hoodoos of Bryce Canyon emerge.

During the uplift the Claron also split into a network of minute fractures. Into these joints rain and snow fell and a shape-shifting force stronger than rock began its inventive work. Summer's thunderous monsoons widened small rifts into deep canyons and rainfall's gentle power hewed columns from thin canyon walls. In winter, snowmelt seeped into tiny crevices, froze, and expanded with enough pressure to pop noses from hoodoos. Bryce Canyon remains a world primed, a realm of stacked potential where every raindrop creates.

Fanciful forms take shape as erosion sculpts the Claron's interbedded layers: sandstones wear most quickly, leaving thin necks; mudstones, more resistant, persist, and limestone endures as bulging waistlines and protruding ribs. Bryce hoodoos bring to mind poodles, gorillas, queens in crinoline, dinosaur heads, and, hey—is that Elvis?

Hoodoos blaze with color when minerals deposited in the Claron's sediments mix with oxygen; iron rusts and manganese waxes blue. Thus, hoodoos blush russet, cinnamon, and the most delicate coral; others effloresce violet, lavender and columbine while untinted limestone burns a creamy white.

FACING PAGE: **Sunrise at Agua Canyon.**

Bryce's myriad colors blend like the soft shades of a naturally dyed Navajo rug—the soft pink of cactus fruit, the warm ivory of natural wool, the bisque of onionskin.

Just as water seeps into myriad pores and fractures the thickness of a lizard's toenail, so life percolates into every niche, colonizing redrock cliffs, defying unstable slopes, wiggling between sand grains. A diverse and lively biotic community animates Bryce.

From the park's highest point at 9,115 feet (2,778 meters) to its lowest at 6,620 feet (2,018 meters) life stacks on life. Plants and animals adapted to Bryce Canyon's lower elevations overcame long ago challenges posed by intense heat and cold, limited nutrients, minuscule precipitation, and loose footing to weave an interactive and unique ecosystem. Scraggly Utah juniper and piñon twist from barren hillsides, sprouting "berries" and nuts appreciated by scrub and pinyon jays. Tree and side-blotched lizards hunt inattentive insects while whipsnakes and garter snakes seek wayward rodents.

Above, in the plateau's mid-elevation ponderosa forests, Merriam's turkeys nibble acorns catered by Gambel oak. Pronghorn, the fastest animal in North America, sprint up to 70 miles-per-hour across upland meadows. Nearby, mule deer and occasional elk browse forest edges as invisible mountain lions watch. Be warned: Unita chipmunks and golden-mantled ground squirrels feel it's their personal duty to greet every visitor, but don't be tempted to feed them: they didn't get those roly-poly bellies from pine nuts!

Bryce Canyon meadows harbor the only protected colony of rare Utah prairie dogs in the world. After years of shooting and poisoning, prairie dog numbers plummeted until even the Bryce colonies disappeared. In the 1970s, the State of Utah reintroduced these rare dogs (actually rodents) to the national park's protection and, by 1995, 200 adults rallied in several colonies. But that year sylvatic plague devastated the colony—

only 11 dogs survived. Plague, a serious disease for both humans and rodents, is a non-native organism unintentionally imported 200 years ago with European rats. Mammals native to the United States have no natural resistance to exotic diseases. Today 300 Utah prairie dogs romp through the meadows of Bryce, but the next epidemic could drive them extinct overnight. For your safety and theirs, please don't venture into prairie dog meadows.

Species adapted to high elevations, like aspen, white fir, and blue spruce, thrive in the strong winds, bright sun, and calamitous snows near Yovimpa Point. Mountain lover, manzanita, and Oregon grape welcome snow's insulating protection. Limber pine flexes in high wind and under heavy snow. Although many animals migrate off the plateau during winter's chill, blue grouse promenade deep drifts while yellow-bellied marmots hibernate below. In summer, white-throated swifts and violet-green swallows rocket over the rim while ravens chuckle amid canyon hoodoos.

One of the world's oldest creatures chooses the worst weather Bryce can conjure. Through snow, heat, or drought the bristlecone pine lives on. One ancient bristlecone anchored to Yovimpa Point celebrates 1,600 years of life. With needled limbs looking like bottlebrushes, bristlecone survives by retaining needles for decades and not creating new ones during dry years.

Although it appears that life struggles in this austere desert, species thrive in fine-tuned niches. When climates change, niches change and geologic layers record mass extinctions. In Bryce the lowest exposed layers chronicle the age of dinosaurs. But in the time expressed in the dust beneath your feet, the largest rate of extinction devastates our world. It's surprising, or perhaps not, that elk, pronghorn, turkey, peregrine falcons, bighorn sheep, prairie dogs and California condors would no longer participate in life's dance at Bryce if they had not been reintroduced after local extinction. Although human-developed recovery programs are one of our best ideas, they cannot keep pace with human-induced extinctions.

From the earliest times, people flowed through Bryce, never lingering more than a season. Native Americans and pioneers moved with the Plateau's rhythms. Snow and bitter cold checked winter habitation while short, dry summers precluded agriculture. Beginning 9,000 years ago a progression of people—Paleo-Indian, Archaic, Fremont, and Paiute—embraced the summer plateau originally hunting now-extinct megafauna then mule deer and prairie dog and gathering cattails, sego lily tubers, and piñon nuts. About 2,500 years ago early puebloans initiated desert agriculture in the Southwest, an experiment continued by first-millennium Anasazi villagers and, in the 1870s, Mormon pioneers. These farmers settled the deserts below, only visiting the plateau to hunt, gather timber, or, in the latter case, graze sheep and cattle.

Although no one lived in Bryce until lodgekeepers and park rangers arrived in the 1920s, under the rim people and towns shuffled across the landscape. In 1847, eager to create a place where Mormons could worship freely, Brigham Young carted his followers beyond the United States into the Utah Territory. Dreaming of a state of Deseret, Young dispatched Mormon pioneers to southern Utah. Between 1874 and 1892 eight settlements sprouted at the Paria's headwaters, but the capricious river rampaged or dried, either way destroying; only Cannonville, Henrieville, and Tropic remain. Typical of many settlers Ebenezer Bryce moved at least 18 times during his life, settling near Cannonville in "Bryce's Canyon" from 1875–1880.

Bryce Canyon hit the big time in 1915 when national forest supervisor J.W. Humphrey rode begrudgingly to the rim and then couldn't be pried away. He opened a visitor's road to Bryce—and we've never stopped coming. Waves of people built lodges, designated a national park, dug trails, and preserved this wondrous place so that today, we can rest in the sanctuary of Bryce Canyon. Below this crockery rim, delicate hoodoos burn in the golden light of evening. To the south, Navajo Mountain rides blue on the horizon, bats flicker in the dusk, and a universe of stars shines overhead like childhood memories.

With a quick glance one might take the sum of Bryce: for-est, meadow, canyon. But naming its parts and processes would take billions of books. One to capture the curve of a raven's bill. Another to name the microbes flourishing in a thimble of soil. One for the sound of a mountain lion breathing. Volumes on the scent of canyons after rain.

Immerse yourself in the wonders of Bryce.

ABOVE: The etched walls of Bryce Canyon below Inspiration Point.

ABOVE: Park visitors enjoy the quiet of the Navajo Loop Trail in winter.

RIGHT: Winter visitors can enjoy snowshoeing or cross-country skiing, as well as more traditional activities. Unlike other parks in the Southwest, temperatures are pleasant in the summer, when Bryce receives the most visitors.

LEFT: Along Fairyland Trail. 60 million years ago a vast fresh water lake covered this area, depositing sediments of varying composition and thickness.

BELOW: The oldest bristlecone pine in Bryce Canyon is found at the edge of Paunsaugunt Plateau near Yovimpa Point. It is estimated to be 1,600 years old.

FACING PAGE: Most of Bryce was logged before it became a national park. Fortunately, *Pinus ponderosa* has made a strong comeback. They grow on dry mountain slopes and mesas from 6,500 to 10,000 feet in elevation.

BELOW: Pines line the open dry wash of Bryce Creek, which floods when heavy rains arrive.

FACING PAGE: Sunrise over Queen's Garden. Some of the sedimentary layers are limestone, some siltstone; all are dyed combinations of red, white, orange, blue, or yellow by minerals, especially iron.

LEFT: The hoodoos give Bryce a surreal atmosphere, sparking many an imagination.

Water erodes rock mechanically
and chemically. Fast-moving water
scrapes its silt, gravel, and rock
debris against firmer bedrock.
Slow-moving water enters minute
rock pores and dissolves cements
holding the rock together.

ABOVE: Golden aspens along the rim drive, near Rainbow Point.

RIGHT: Mule deer are blue-gray in winter and reddish in summer. ART WOLFE

FACING PAGE: Manzanita bushes and pines along lower portion of Navajo Loop Trail.

ABOVE: Paria View is carved of rocks that lie deep beneath the Paunsaugunt Plateau, the edge of which is now exposed to erosion.

RIGHT: In Bryce, erosion happens relatively quickly. More than 200 times a year ice forms overnight and thaws the next morning.

ABOVE: A Douglas fir grows in the Wall Street section of the fairly strenuous Navajo Loop Trail.

RIGHT: Early morning light in the Agua Canyon.

FACING PAGE: There are only three aspen trees inside the rim of the canyon, though forests abound behind the rim. DAVID MUENCH

RIGHT: Tropic Ditch flows from the East Fork of the Sevier River.

FACING PAGE: Evergreens manage to take hold on the steep slopes along Peek-a-Boo Trail.

In winter, prevailing winds from the northwest help determine where snow will settle.

LEFT: Hikers enjoy the scenic beauty of Fairyland Canyon. Sun protection and drinking water are essentials on summer jaunts.

BELOW: Ponderosa pines are easily recognized by their tall, straight, thick trunks, with rusty-orange bark smelling of vanilla.

RIGHT: One of the cabins available for rent near the canyon rim.

BELOW: Ponderosa pine cones and manzanita leaves on the canyon floor.

FACING PAGE: Ponderosa pines grow straight and tall on the canyon floor.

BELOW: Summer grasses in open meadow along the canyon rim.

ABOVE: Bryce Amphitheater from Sunrise Point.

RIGHT: If you don't mind cold, winter is a beautiful time to visit Bryce.

FACING PAGE: Spires and turrets along the Peek-a-Boo Loop Trail.

RIGHT: View from Bryce Point area. Bryce Canyon is named for pioneer Ebenezer Bryce who came to the valley with his family in 1875.

BELOW: Wild turkeys run to avoid danger. They roost in trees along the canyon rim.
TOM AND PAT LEESON

FACING PAGE: An archway along the Peek-a-Boo Trail.
Erosion eventually collapses archways.

BELOW: The Silent City from Inspiration Point.

LEFT: Bryce Canyon is one of the most beautiful places on the Colorado Plateau. This is a section of the Navajo Loop Trail.

BELOW: Indian Paintbrush typically blooms in July and August.

RIGHT: In the 1920s, homesteaders Reuben and Minnie Syrett brought their friends to see the stone formations at Bryce. Soon they developed sleeping and eating facilities on the canyon rim.

BELOW: Golden-mantled ground squirrels are common inhabitants in the canyon. They feed on seeds, fruits, insects, eggs, and meat.

ABOVE: Bryce Canyon National Park was officially designated on February 25, 1928.

LEFT: Limestone formations stand like ships in a sea of evergreens near Rainbow Point.

RIGHT: Hoodoos reach skyward along canyon floor.

BELOW: Natural sandstone arch along Navajo Trail.

ABOVE: A small hoodoo remnant along Bryce Creek wash on the canyon floor.

LEFT: Of the three great Southwest canyons—Grand, Zion, and Bryce—Bryce is the youngest geologically.

ABOVE: Knarled bristlecone pine along Queens Garden Trail.

FACING PAGE: The forces of erosion may be nowhere more evident than at Bryce.
In 50 years the present rim will be cut back into the plateau another foot.

Early morning twilight over the canyon shows the muted shades of color that will soon intensify with firest sunlight.

RIGHT: Bryce Canyon winters are cold; at park headquarters the temperature falls below zero an average of 21 days per year.

BELOW: Paria View looks across hoodoos south to the White Cliffs.

FACING PAGE: White Cliffs near Ponderosa Canyon.

RIGHT: Coyote is a frequently depicted character in myth and legend of the Southwest. According to the Paiutes, it was coyote who changed the people into stone in the canyon. ART WOLFE

BELOW: Foxtails bow in the wind.

RIGHT: Ponderosa pine hides among limestone formation in Queen's Garden. The 1.8-mile Queen's Garden Trail is marked with signposts giving information on the area's geology and stories about how the formations got their names.

LEFT: Golden asters along the canyon rim.

BELOW: Bryce is home to the Utah prairie dog, one of five prairie dog species that inhabit North America. Its range is limited to the southwestern quarter of Utah. ART WOLFE

LEFT: Bryce Canyon Lodge offers dining and lodging for visitors.

BELOW: Bristlecone pines are found throughout the Great Basin in the western United States. The average age of bristlecones is about 1,000 years, with a few more than 4,000 years old. Very young bristlecones also live in the park.

RIGHT: In Bryce, conditions are optimal for erosion—steep slopes increase water speed and energy.

BELOW: Debris carried by runoff scours softer rock and creates gullies, while harder rock remains as fins.

ABOVE: A tributary of Sevier Creek fed by Tropic Ditch.

LEFT: Eroded limestone cliffs near Rainbow Point. A scenic drive
along the rim ascends more than 1,000 feet to Rainbow Point.

RIGHT: Rolling hills of the Claron Formation near 8,076-foot-tall Boat Mesa.

BELOW: A pine tree clings to a slope below the hoodoos along the Queen's Garden Trail.

FAR LEFT: Natural bridge overlook.

LEFT: Hikers descend into the depths of Bryce Canyon on Navajo Loop Trail. A hike is a great way to explore the canyon.

ABOVE: Steller's jays are often very bold near human habitation.
TOM AND PAT LEESON

RIGHT: A waterfall in Water Canyon pours over a sandstone ledge.

ABOVE: Ponderosa pines in a snow-covered meadow.

LEFT: Paiutes lived in the area when Capt. Clarence E. Dutton explored here in the 1870s.

The Hunter hoodoo in Agua Canyon. Now and then a boulder topples from its perch.

FACING PAGE: The Visitor Center with museum displays, gift shop, and interpretive center.

LEFT: At Bryce it is easy to see creation in destruction, beauty in the cycle of freeze and thaw.

BELOW: Most of the golden eagle's prey is taken on the ground—sometimes it hunts while soaring at great heights, with its wings held horizontally. ART WOLFE

James Randklev

Master landscape photographer James Randklev has photographed America for thirty years, primarily with a large-format camera that provides the rich images collected in this volume. His brilliant and sensitive work has made him one of the Sierra Club's most published photographers. His color photographs have appeared in books, periodicals, calendars, and advertising—and have been exhibited in shows in the United States and abroad. In 1997, he was the sole American chosen to exhibit in the International Exhibition of Nature Photography in Evian, France. In 2003 Randklev was selected to be included in a book titled "World's Top Nature Photographers—and the stories behind their greatest images" by Roto Vision Publications, London, England. His photography books are *Arizona Impressions; Monterey Peninsula Impressions; Tucson Impressions; Zion National Park Impressions; In Nature's Heart: The Wilderness Days of John Muir; Georgia: Images of Wildness; Wild and Scenic Florida; Georgia Impressions; Georgia Simply Beautiful; Olympic National Park Impressions; Florida Impressions,* and *Florida Simply Beautiful.*

More of James Randklev's imagery can be view at www.JamesRandklev.com.

© MICHAEL HELMS

Greer K. Chesher

Award-winning author Greer Chesher travels the Southwest with her faithful companion Bo, the border collie, in search of truth, vision, and a good cuppa coffee. She rangered for the National Park Service for 20 years at such wondrous places as Zion and Grand Canyon National Parks, Santa Monica Mountains National Recreation Area, and Bandelier National Monument.

Her book *Heart of the Desert Wild: Grand Staircase—Escalante National Monument* won the Utah Book Award for Nonfiction and the National Association of Interpreters' Book of the Year Award. Her book *Dinosaur: The Dinosaur National Monument Quarry* came in second for the same award. Greer's other books include: *The Desert's Hoodoo Heart: Bryce Canyon National Park,* and *The Mighty Stage Remains, Filmmaking on the High Plateaus.* Her articles have appeared in *Northern Lights, Petroglyph, and Canon Journal.*

Greer lives in Rockville, Utah, and follows where curiosity leads, writing all the way.